A Study of Dual Enrollment and Low-Income and Minority Students

A Study of Dual Enrollment and Low-Income and Minority Students

A Dissertation

Submitted to the
Faculty of Argosy University Sarasota
College of Education

In partial Fulfillment of
The Requirements for the Degree of

Doctor of Education

Gail Laurel Johnson

Copyright © 2013 by Gail Laurel Johnson.

Library of Congress Control Number:		2013918530
ISBN:	Hardcover	978-1-4931-1369-9
	Softcover	978-1-4931-1368-2
	Ebook	978-1-4931-1370-5

All rights reserved. No part of this book may be reproduced or transmitted in any form or by any means, electronic or mechanical, including photocopying, recording, or by any information storage and retrieval system, without permission in writing from the copyright owner.

This book was printed in the United States of America.

Rev. date: 10/24/2013

To order additional copies of this book, contact:
Xlibris LLC
1-888-795-4274
www.Xlibris.com
Orders@Xlibris.com
142690

A STUDY OF DUAL ENROLLMENT AND LOW-INCOME
AND MINORITY STUDENTS

A Dissertation

Submitted to the
Faculty of Argosy University Sarasota
College of Education

In partial Fulfillment of
The Requirements for the Degree of

Doctor of Education

By

Gail Laurel Johnson

Argosy University

April, 2009

Dissertation Committee Approval:

_____   _____
Ronald Kar, PhD., Chair   Date

_____
Larry Gay Reagan, Ed.,D., Member

_____   _____
Kenneth Rometo, Ed.D., Member   Program Chair

A STUDY OF DUAL ENROLLMENT AND LOW-INCOME
AND MINORITY STUDENTS

Abstract of Dissertation

Submitted to the
Faculty of Argosy University
College of Education

In Partial Fulfillment of
The Requirements for the Degree of

Doctor of Education

By

Gail Laurel Johnson

Argosy University

April, 2009

Chair: Dr. Ronald Kar, PhD

Committee: Larry Gay Reagan, Ed.D.

Kenneth Rometo, Ed.D.

Department: College of Education

Contents

CHAPTER ONE: THE PROBLEM AND ITS COMPONENTS 21
Introduction 21
Problem Background 23
Literature Review 24
Introduction 24
    Benefits of Dual Enrollment Program 24
    Criticisms of the Dual Enrollment Program 25
Purpose of the Study 25
Research Questions 26
Limitations/Delimitations 26
    Limitations 26
    Delimitations 26
Definitions 26
Significance of the Study 27

CHAPTER TWO: REVIEW OF THE LITERATURE 29
Introduction 29
History of Acceleration Options Programs 30
Dual Enrollment Program 31
    Benefits of Dual Enrollment 32
    Criticisms of Dual Enrollment Programs 33
Variations in Dual Enrollment Programs across the States 34
Financing Dual Enrollment Programs 36
    Admissions Requirements 37
    Target Populations 38
    Program Intensity 38
    Course Content 38
    Instructors 39
    Student Mix and Location 39
    Credits 39
    State Policy 39
The Impact of Accelerated Options on Minority Students 40
Summary 40

CHAPTER THREE: METHODOLOGY 42
INTRODUCTION 42
RESEARCH DESIGN 43
Selection of Participants 43
Instrumentation 43
PROCEDURES 44
DATA PROCESSING AND ANALYSIS 44

CHAPTER FOUR: FINDINGS 45
RESTATEMENT OF THE PURPOSE 45
RESEARCH QUESTION 1 46
RESEARCH QUESTION 2 48
RESEARCH QUESTION 3 50
INTERVIEW 52
ARCHIVAL DATA 53

CHAPTER FIVE: SUMMARY, CONCLUSIONS, AND RECOMMENDATIONS 56
SUMMARY 56
CONCLUSIONS 58
IMPLICATIONS FOR PRACTICE 61
IMPLICATIONS FOR RESEARCH 61
RECOMMENDATIONS 62

REFERENCES 63

APPENDIXES

APPENDIX A: SURVEY 69

APPENDIX B: INTERVIEW 73

Tables

Table 4.1—Survey Question 6 47

Table 4.2—Survey Question 7 47

Table 4.3—Survey Question 8 48

Table 4.4—Survey Question 9 49

Table 4.5—Survey Question 10 49

Table 4.6—Survey Question 12 51

Table 4.7—Survey Question 11 51

Table 4.8—Dual Enrollment Penetration Study by College 54

Table 4.9—Dual Enrollment Rates of Penetration by Race/Ethnicity 55

DEDICATION

In the name of Jesus the Christ, I want to give thanks and praise to God, the Father, the Son, and the Holy Spirit for being there for me, and with me at all times. I could not do this without you, Lord.

I would also like to dedicate this Doctorate to my deceased husband Dr. Edwin S. Johnson, who thought that it was my destiny to accomplish this goal; to my beautiful daughter Laurel L Johnson; and to my deceased mother Grace Y. Fermin, who always believed that education was the key that would open many doors for her children.

I want to especially, thank, my dear friend Sue Sunderman, my Technological Advisor on this project for her unwavering support, prayers, and encouragement. You are a true friend in deed, and in need. I also want to thank Jillian Lewis-Darden, Jeanne Silvester, Renita Williams, Doris Howard, my sister Sandra V. Noel, Mary Streck and the rest of my family and friends for all their support and prayers. Thank you all very much.

Author Bio

Gail L. Johnson

Gail L. Johnson is an Assistant Professor at the University of the Southern Caribbean in the School of Education and Human Sciences in Trinidad and Tobago. Dr. Johnson's teaching experience includes educational leadership, school law, finance and marketing, principles of educational supervision, and psychology of learning and instruction. Prior to moving to the University, she taught mathematics, science and American history in high school in the United States. Dr Johnson also served for seven years with distinction, as a Meteorologist in the United States Air Force.

Dr. Johnson received her doctorate from Argosy University in Educational Leadership. Her bachelor's degree is in Health Care Management from Southern Illinois University, and her master's degree is in Educational Leadership from Argosy University.

Abstract

This study investigated the impact of the Dual Enrollment Program on the academic achievement of low-income and minority high school students, in a coastal district in a southern state. Bridging the gap between high school and college is the ultimate goal of this program. The study focused on how students find out, about the program, their participation, and success rate, in the program. A survey was sent to high school guidance counselors, and a few of them completed it. They indicated that students were informed about the program through teachers, administrators, guidance counselors, school postings, and letters sent home to parents. A telephone interview was conducted with Personnel from the Community college, and Archival data were examined.

The results of the study revealed that there was a small percentage of minority students participating in the program, compared to white students. It also indicated that minority students who participated in the program were successful, and went on to college. There was reluctance on the part of many guidance counselors to respond to the surveys, even after repeated requests from their Supervisors. Community College personnel pointed out, that recent increased efforts had been made to promote the DE Program in the district.

Acknowledgements

This has been a very long journey for me, fraught with ups, and downs, and twists and turns. Through it all, I had the constant support and commitment from my dedicated and wonderful advisor, and chair, Dr. Ronald Kar. I could not have done this Doctoral Program without your help. I want to sincerely thank you for encouraging me, and sticking with me the entire time. Without your expertise and proper direction, this study would not have been possible. I am sorry if I turned your brown hair white, but I am ever grateful for all that you have done for me in this process. Thank you again.

I would also like to thank Dr. Larry Gay Reagan, second chair, and Dr. Kenneth Rometo for their invaluable support and contributions in this venture.

Chapter One

THE PROBLEM AND ITS COMPONENTS

Introduction

This study investigated the impact of a dual enrollment program on the academic achievement of low-income and minority students. Specifically it sought to answer three questions:

Research Question 1: How do low-income and minority high school students find out about the Dual Enrollment Program available to them?
Research Question 2: To what extent do low-income and minority high school students participate in their local Dual Enrollment Program?
Research Question 3: What is the success rate of low-income and minority high school students in their local Dual Enrollment Program?

With the inevitability of globalization, there is an increasing demand for well-educated and technologically proficient innovators. Not so long ago a high school diploma was considered sufficient for young people to enter the workforce. Today, it would be prudent to say that some form of postsecondary education is required to compete for a fair amount of the highest paying, fastest growing occupations in our society, according to Krueger, (2006).

According to researchers Walthers and Robinson (2006), "preparing students for the transition from the high school environment to the college campus is becoming an increasingly important goal of policy makers and educators" (p. 2). Educators have created a variety of programs including acceleration options programs to assist students with this transition. The Dual Enrollment Program is one such acceleration option program designed to bridge the gap between high school and college.

According to the Education Commission of the States (2001):

> The standard definition of a dual or concurrent enrollment is defined as a high school student enrolled in a postsecondary institution while still in high school. Differing definitions of dual or concurrent enrollment have been so noted.
>
> Types of dual/concurrent enrollment:
> Standard Dual/Concurrent Enrollment Programs: Allow high school students to enroll in postsecondary courses usually for credit. Generally students are taught by college faculty, either at the college or high school, or through distance education.
> College High Programs: Agreements between high schools and postsecondary institutions to offer college-level courses at the high school, typically for credit (secondary, postsecondary or both secondary and postsecondary credit). Curriculum content and standards are determined by the postsecondary institution, while courses are typically taught by high school faculty who hold the same credentials as postsecondary faculty.
> Tech Prep or 2 + 2 Programs: These programs provide an articulated high school/community college curriculum for professional or technical fields. The courses often reduce duplication between high school and college, thereby helping students to move seamlessly between the systems. Courses may be taught either by high school or community college staff. (p. 4)

The dual enrollment program rewards motivated students by letting them preview college life while still in high school, and saving them money at the same time. In fact, the logic behind the program is that students would begin to build a college transcript, while still in high school. Researcher Windham (1997) contends "the dual enrollment option was established to enrich the course opportunities for outstanding high school students and to provide an acceleration mechanism that would move students through the baccalaureate degree process quicker" (p. 9). Dual enrollment programs are now found in 47 states throughout the nation (Krueger, 2006), and policymakers, the academic community and parents have come to view this program as another option in educational acceleration.

Problem Background

Krueger (2006) contends that there is a perception that the targeted population for dual enrollment programs is not low-income and other underrepresented students, who may benefit from it the most, but students who are academically successful. In addition, Kruger notes that "schools with the highest minority enrollment were the least likely to offer dual enrollment courses when compared to schools with lower minority enrollment" (p.3). Another researcher Kazis (2004), also stated "that the fastest growing segments of most states' populations—in school and in the work force—are those groups that have the greatest academic disadvantages: minorities, new immigrants, youth from low-income families" (p. 5). Kazis (2004) further noted that:

> "the high school graduation rates of the fastest growing population groups lag significantly. While more than three out of four white and Asian American youth graduated from high school after four years, the graduation rate for African Americans is only 55 percent and for Hispanics, 53 percent" (p. 5).

According to Hoffman (2005), the high school graduation rate in Florida is one of the lowest in the nation. She stated that "Florida ranks 49th in the number of students completing high school" (p.17), but the state dual enrollment program is one of the best in the nation, according to Hoffman and Robins (2005).

Hoffman and Robbins further state that:

> Florida has the nation's most highly articulated and centralized public system in the country, and its dual enrollment legislation mandates that all 28 community colleges and specific four-year institutions participate. Required local partnership agreements spell out the division of responsibilities in regard to books, transportation, advising, and support. The program is accepted as a path to college for middle achievers and students on a career/technical track, as well as for students classified as gifted (p.6).

According to Florida's Dual Enrollment Program (2006), "the purpose of the Dual Enrollment (DE) program is to broaden the scope of the high school curricula, increase the depth of high school study, and shorten the time to college degree" (Florida's Dual Enrollment Program, p.1). There are partnerships between local school districts and post secondary institutions, which allow high school students to enroll in college courses and to use those courses for high school credit. The staff members who teach dual enrollment courses are approved to teach college-level courses, and they may be either high school teachers or college faculty members (Florida's Dual Enrollment Program, 2006).

Participating in the Dual Enrollment program has positive outcomes for low-income and underrepresented students. Researchers Horne and Armstrong (2004), in Florida contend that "Hispanic and African American students who took Dual Enrollment courses are enrolling in higher education at higher rates than white or any other ethnic groups" (p. 1). Horne and Armstrong (2006) also found "that students with DE experience maintained a higher (SUS) GPA than those who had not participated in DE (p. 3).

Literature Review

Introduction

"Senioritis" or student disengagement is a growing problem in schools, especially during the last two years of high school (Andrews & Davis, 2003). It seems that some students are not challenged enough when they enter their junior and senior years in high school, so they get bored and sometimes drop out of school. Educators are constantly seeking ways to address and correct this problem. A practical solution to student disengagement in high school is the dual enrollment program. This program presents students the opportunity to build a college transcript with stimulating and challenging coursework, exposes high school students to college life, saves students and their family's money, and creates partnerships between high schools and colleges that formalize articulation between these institutions (Boswell, 2001; Helfgot, 2001; Hoffman, 2003; Windham, 1997).

Although the program is geared towards attracting motivated high achieving students (Krueger, 2006), its concepts encompass all students, especially the low-income and underserved. According to Hugo (2001), when given the opportunity to participate in the dual enrollment program, students from this minority group are "enlightened, committed and keenly aware of the potential benefits offered through dual enrollment—students are exposed to college life, and this instills in them the awareness that they are capable, erudite individuals who can achieve a great deal" (p.69).

Benefits of Dual Enrollment Program

Since its inception in the early 1970's the dual/concurrent program has been beneficial to students in many different ways. Besides being academically challenging, which in itself is a stimulant and a solution to boredom and disengagement in school, the dual enrollment program allows students to earn college credits towards an Associate of Arts degree or an Associate of Science degree, according to Andrews and Davis (2003). Students and their families save additional money because the textbooks and other materials required for courses are paid for by the districts. College credits that are earned through the dual enrollment program are free and transferable to state colleges throughout the state of Florida (Hebert, 2001). Hebert (2001) further contends that postsecondary institutions inherit bright students who have had experience with the college environment, which minimizes remediation courses in college and increases the potential for graduation. The result, this researcher says, is the graduation of capable, educated, and invaluable individuals, who are ready to compete in the global marketplace.

Criticisms of the Dual Enrollment Program

Some researchers have raised concerns about the Dual Enrollment Program. According to Boswell, (2001) and Hebert (2001), transferring credits earned in the program, to private institutions can be problematic for students. While state run colleges and universities accept these credits, private institutions will not. The reasoning behind this is that some officials in private institutions doubt the credibility of high school teachers and the quality of the courses they teach to students enrolled in the dual enrollment program, on high school campuses. Boswell (2001) stated that "the excessive workload for the high school teachers selected to teach the college-level courses, as well as the perception that the college curriculum needs to be "dumbed down" in order to be accessible to high school students" (p. 11), are the main reasons for the concerns. Other concerns, according to researchers include inequitable access to the program for low-income, and minority students (Krueger, 2006). And for state policymakers, the "double-dipping" impact on taxpayers when both K-12 districts and community colleges receive state support for secondary students concurrently enrolled in postsecondary classes" (Boswell, 2001, p. 11).

Purpose of the Study

The purpose of the study was to investigate the Dual Enrollment Program in a Coastal School District in a southern state hereafter referred to as CSD, and to determine the impact the program was having on the academic achievement of low-income and other minority high school students in terms of their access to the program, their participation in the program, and their success rate while enrolled in the program.

Research Questions

Research Question 1: How do low-income and minority high school students find out about the Dual Enrollment Program available to them?
Research Question 2: To what extent do low-income and minority high school students participate in their local Dual Enrollment Program?
Research Question 3: What is the success rate of low-income and minority high school students in their local Dual Enrollment Program?

Limitations/Delimitations

Limitations

The survey used in this study was constructed by the researcher after being reviewed for content/construct validity by a group of non-participant professionals. It was not tested outside the Coastal School District. There was no guarantee that the participants would complete the survey accurately and without bias. Participants' knowledge was limited to procedures and academic offerings within their school environments. The study was conducted at five high schools in a Coastal School District in a southern state, using the guidance counselors of these schools as survey participants.

Delimitations

This study was conducted in a small Coastal School District, in a southern state, and involved five public high schools. Archived data for high school students, who are eligible and meet the requirements to participate in acceleration option programs, was also examined to observe trends. The population was selected because of convenience and within the researcher's ability to manage. Due to the small sample, the results of this study cannot be generalized to that of guidance counselors in other school districts.

Definitions

The following terms were defined as they were used in this study.
Acceleration mechanisms. For the purpose of this study, this term refers to the opportunity to move ahead or pursue a higher level of education (Hoffman, 2005).

Advanced Placement. This term refers to courses offered at high schools and taught by high school faculty. The courses are designed and overseen by the College Board. Students may earn high school credit and college credit simultaneously (Smith, 2003).

Dual Enrollment. This term refers to a partnership between high schools and colleges that allows high school students to enroll in college courses while concurrently enrolled in high school. Students receive credit toward a high school diploma and a college degree for dual enrollment courses as provided in the institutions' articulation agreement (Hebert, 2001, Definitions section ¶ 3).

Early College High School. This term refers to small autonomous schools that blend high school and college into a coherent educational program (Jobs for the Future, 2004).

Low-income. This term refers to an individual whose family's taxable income for the preceding year did not exceed 150 percent of the poverty level amount. The poverty level is equal to $31,800 per annum for a family unit of four, in 48 Contiguous States, excluding Alaska and Hawaii (U S Department of Health and Human Services, 2008).

Senioritis. This term refers to a period in high school when students become bored or disengaged, because they feel they are not challenged enough (Andrews & Davis, 2003).

Underrepresented students. This term refers to students of color, first-generation college goers, and students whose first language is not English (Kazis, 2004).

Significance of the Study

Research has indicated that the majority of students dropping out of high school come from the underrepresented populations, students of color, students whose first language is not English, and students from low-income families (Kazis, 2004). Students seem to be bored and disengaged, mainly in the eleventh and twelfth grades due to repetition of coursework, poor curriculum design, watered down courses, and lack of connectivity with faculty (Andrews & Davis, 2003). Dual Enrollment programs are a proven vehicle for increasing student high school completion among minority and low-income populations. Acquiring college credits while in high school also saves on college tuition, enabling students to finish an undergraduate degree faster and with less indebtedness.

While there are many reasons why dual enrollment programs are helpful, the question remains why certain groups are underrepresented in dual enrollment programs. This particular study looked at what guidance counselors said about minority and low-income students' knowledge, access and success in their dual enrollment programs.

This study also provided insight into the viability and use of this acceleration option as a tool for challenging and graduating high school students, while preparing them for college life and a postsecondary education.

Chapter Two

REVIEW OF THE LITERATURE

This study investigated the impact of a dual enrollment program on the academic achievement of low-income and minority students. This review of the literature related to dual enrollment was organized under the topics of the three research questions that guided this study.

Research Question 1: How do low-income and minority high school students find out about the Dual Enrollment Program available to them?
Research Question 2: To what extent do low-income and minority high school students participate in their local Dual Enrollment Program?
Research Question 3: What is the success rate of low-income and minority high school students in their local Dual Enrollment Program?

Introduction

Dual enrollment partnerships began in the late 1970s between high schools and colleges throughout the United States (Hebert, 2001). The emergence of these partnerships created opportunities that challenge the intellectual faculties of motivated high school students, and provide them with engaging opportunities that ultimately prepare them for the transition from high school to college (Andrews & Davis, 2003; Botstein, 2006; Hebert, 2001).

Researchers have identified a problem of student disengagement in high school, most noticeably during the junior and senior years (Andrews and Davis 2003; Blanchard, 1971; Botstein, 2006; Hoffman & Robins,

2005). They say poor curriculum design, redundancy, repetition, and a lack of connectivity between students and faculty account for a major portion of this ongoing problem. Existing pedagogical approaches are in constant competition with advances in technology, especially the internet, which plays a major role in how adolescents communicate in our society today (Botstein, 2006). Collaborative efforts between colleges and high schools promoting the dual enrollment programs provide rigor and sustainability to courses that essentially arouse and engage the curiosity of high achieving motivated high school students (Boswell, 2001; Clark, 2001; Helfgot, 2001).

Boswell (2001) tells us that "a highly educated and trained workforce to compete in an increasingly global economy" (p. 8) is the goal of policymakers and politicians. A summary of acceleration options for high school student including Advance Placement, Early College High Schools, and Dual Enrollment Programs follows.

History of Acceleration Options Programs

The College Board first established "early college admissions programs" (Boswell, 2001, p. 8) in the 1950's. The programs were used to "encourage educational acceleration" (Boswell, 2001, p. 8) at that time. The Advanced Placement (AP) and the College Level Examination Program (CLEP) were part of the initial package

The AP courses allow "secondary students to take college-level courses while still in high school" (Boswell, 2001, p. 8). When completed students take a national exam. If they receive a passing grade on the exam, colleges and universities gave them advanced standing, that is, course credit, when they were accepted at these institutions. On the other hand, students who passed exams on beginning level college courses through CLEP (College Level Examination Program), were given college and university level credits for these courses (Boswell, 2001; Smith, 2003).

A few years later a high rate of reported failures in high school and student disengagement, better known as "senioritis" prompted the Carnegie Commission (1971) to recommend "structural changes in the United States system of higher education" (Hebert, 2001, Literature Review section, ¶ 1). Suggested reforms included improvements in teacher preparation and strategies, cutting out either one year of high school or one year of college, making a three-year bachelor's degree program, and giving college credit to coursework done by seniors in high schools. Part of the problem was attributed to repetition in coursework and overlap of material in high schools and colleges (Carnegie Commission On Higher Education, 1971). Project Advance emerged at Syracuse University, and the Dual Enrollment Program began.

Another acceleration option program emerged in the 1980's called the International Baccalaureate Program. The curriculum is very strict, and runs for four years. The program is "designed for highly motivated high school students" (Boswell, 2001, p. 8). An IB diploma is awarded to students on successful completion of the program; and when they are admitted to post secondary institutions, they receive advance standing at these institutions.

In 2002, the Early College High School was established. This is an alternative form of high school. The objective of these small schools is to "blend high school and the first two years of college, with the goal of moving low-income and poorly prepared students toward the Associate's or Bachelor's degree in fewer than the six years it would normally take to get from grades 9 through 14" (Hoffman & Vargas, 2005, p. 3). Early College High Schools are usually found on, or near college campuses, and have been funded by the Bill and Melinda Gates Foundation, the Carnegie Corporation of New York, the Ford Foundation, and the W.K. Kellogg Foundation (Hoffman & Vargas, 2005). The plan is to establish 170 ECHS by the year 2008.

Dual Enrollment Program

The 1971 Carnegie Commission on Higher Education's focus was on reform in pedagogy and curriculum, which was later widely discussed and researched during the 1970's, because the rate of student failure in high schools was escalating. The implications were that students were bored and turned off by high school, due to repetition in curriculum content, poor teaching, and redundancy. The academic community was again searching for answers to combat this reoccurring problem (Andrews & Davis, 2003; Blanchard, 1971; Botstein, 2006; Hoffman & Robins, 2005). Then in 1972, Syracuse University experimented with a program called Project Advance, in which a University was partnered with local high schools. College courses were taught on high school campuses by high school faculty, who also held positions as university faculty (Education Commission of the States, 2001; Smith, 2003). It was the first of its kind. The experiment proved to be successful, and the dual enrollment program began in the United States (Education Commission of the States, 2001; Smith, 2003).

It became apparent, that dual enrollment was a key component in motivating students, while meeting their academic needs. According to researchers Gehring (2001) and Vargas (2004), the program attracts a more diverse student population than the AP program and gives credence to the notion of education reform. The program exposes students to interesting and challenging options in courses that could be used towards a bachelor's degree;

and it also attracts more students from low income backgrounds, while giving them the opportunity to experience college campus life, making transitioning from high school to college that much easier (Bailey, Hughes & Karp, 2004; Hoffman & Robbins, 2005; Hugo, 2001).

Benefits of Dual Enrollment

According to Krueger (2006), "there is evidence that dual enrollment increases academic performance and educational attainment" (p. 2). Researchers Bailey, Hughes, and Karp (2003) have found that the dual enrollment program offers motivated students, who are ready for challenges and academic arousal, more curricula options from which to choose. It engages them intellectually and refocuses their natural inquisitiveness in subject areas that hold their interest. Another report suggest that "dual enrollment students performed equally as well as regular college students in subsequent coursework and once in college, maintained as high or higher grade point averages as all other transfer students" (Hebert, 2001, Literature Review section ¶ 4). After participating in the dual enrollment program, students are more prepared academically and socially for the transition to and the rigors of college life (Bailey, Hughes & Karp; 2003; Smith, 2003).

Hoffman and Robins (2005) contend, that during the junior and senior years in high school, dually enrolled students can "earn up to two year's worth of tuition-free college credit" (p. 3), which shortens the time to a college degree. Krueger (2006) also stated that, "college credits earned prior to high school graduation reduce the average time-to-degree and increase the likelihood of graduation for the students who participate in these programs" (p. 1).

Another significant advantage to students and parents is the savings in the cost of college tuition. College credits earned through the program can be transferred to colleges and universities that are in partnership with high schools. The savings can add up to thousands of dollars for most families, (Boswell, 2001; Hoffman & Robins, 2005).

Having qualified high school faculty members teach courses in the dual enrollment program can be an advantage. The best teachers become part of the program and this is an attraction that draws motivated students into the classes they teach (Helfgot, 2001).

When teaching on the high school campus is not a viable option, courses offered on college campuses help students integrate into college campus life. According to Bailey, Hughes and Karp (2003), "exposure to the non-academic side of college, can serve as a demystifying experience for students and ease the psychological transition to college" (p. 2).

Researcher Krueger (2006), also found that states are inclined to create dual enrollment programs for various reasons to include: "Fostering relationships between high schools and colleges, enhancing the efficiency of K-12 and postsecondary systems; implementing a rigorous college-prep curriculum for all; increasing postsecondary attainment rates; reducing the number of students in remediation" (p. 3).

Overall, politicians, academicians, and families are all supportive of dual enrollment programs for various reasons. For the politicians, it gives them "a highly educated and trained workforce to compete in an increasingly global marketplace" (Boswell, 2001, p. 8). Academicians are excited because they believe "they are improving students' educational opportunities and quality of life" (Gomez, 2001, p. 81), while keeping them engaged through a rigorous and challenging program. Families benefit from substantial savings for college tuition. And a wide range of students are given the opportunity to go on to complete a postsecondary education, and in most cases remedial courses in college are not required, due to students' preparedness (Boswell, 2001).

Criticisms of Dual Enrollment Programs

Researchers and policymakers have noted that low-income and low achieving high school students are not always included in dual enrollment programs (Bailey, Hughes, Fermin & Karp, 2005). In order to maintain program quality, eligibility requirements for enrollment into many programs are designed for academically advanced students. Specifications such as grade point average, SAT and ACT scores, teacher recommendation, and standard placement tests are some of the criteria used for student selection. Restrictive policies sometimes exclude students who may need encouragement in attending college or who are bored with traditional high school. However, Krueger, (2006), notes, "that when students are challenged, they achieve at higher levels" (p.2). States like Ohio and Florida try to accommodate a broad range of students without jeopardizing the quality of the programs (Bailey, Fermin, Hughes & Karp, 2005).

The dual enrollment program is criticized for the qualification of high school teachers who teach college-level courses. The implication is that students are not receiving college-level instruction. Although, many of these high school teachers simultaneously teach at universities and colleges as adjunct faculty, it is still a controversial issue to many in academia (Hebert, 2001). National certification for instructors has yet to be determined (Bailey, Fermin, Hughes & Karp, 2005).

Another important area of contention in the dual enrollment program is the transfer of credits earned by students. There is no specific set of national data or rules that govern the entire systems of dual enrollment. What is acceptable in one state is not necessarily acceptable in another state. For instance, in the State of Florida, dual enrollment courses are taught in all 28 community colleges and some four-year colleges. As noted by Krueger (2006), "college credit earned in high school will transfer to any public college or university" (p. 3), in that state. There is no guarantee that colleges and universities in other states will accept transfer credits from Florida and vice versa (Brush, 2005; Greenberg, 1989), requiring Florida students who want to attend colleges in other states to conduct research on courses that they intend to take in the dual enrollment program to make sure they will be accepted: the objective being to determine beforehand, the courses that can be taken in high school that will later earn them credit at the colleges or universities of their choice.

Variations in Dual Enrollment Programs across the States

Terminology associated with dual enrollment may differ from one state to another; but "the curriculum content and standards are determined by the appropriate academic department" (Boswell, 2001, p. 8) of the two or four year accredited colleges associated with the program. Typically, the dual enrollment courses are offered to high school students in two ways. Faculty members with the same academic credentials can teach the courses in high schools as college faculty. Alternatively, college faculty can teach the courses on college campuses (Bailey, Hughes & Karp, 2003). Credit earned from these courses can be used simultaneously towards a high school diploma or college degree. In some cases dual enrollment courses can be obtained through the internet to accommodate students who live in rural areas, or students who are being home schooled (Bailey, Hughes & Karp, 2003; Boswell, 2001). Students participating in the program are challenged academically, and the No Child Left Behind Act is satisfied in the area of "encouraging greater academic rigor during the high school experience" (The High School Leadership Summit, 2005, p.1).

According to Krueger (2006):

> The following states represent a cross-section of program designs and outcomes.:
> Florida: Most college courses in Florida are available for dual enrollment. Legislation mandates that all 28 community colleges and certain four-year institutions offer dual enrollment opportunities. In most cases, the college credit earned in high school will transfer to any public college or university. Students

who attend a Florida public college or university are exempt from paying registration, matriculation, or laboratory fees for courses taken through dual enrollment. Florida's data collection system can follow students through the high-school-to-college pipeline to determine where achievement gaps exist.

Minnesota: Established in 1985, the *Postsecondary Enrollment Options Program* was the first dual enrollment program in the United States. Minnesota statute makes the offering of dual enrollment options mandatory. Students pay no tuition or associated costs. The state has also set participation guidelines that specify students may not take more than the equivalent of two years of coursework through the program and schools may not offer students developmental or remedial coursework. It is estimated that, during the 2004-05 school year, 7441 Minnesota high school juniors and seniors participated in PSEO at a postsecondary institution while 14,000 students participated in college-level course taught at a high school. A University of Minnesota study estimates the number of students taking Advanced Placement tests in the state between 1986 and 2004 increased by 98% because of the PSEO program.

New York: There is no state dual enrollment legislation in New York. However, the City University of New York (CUNY) and the New York Department of Education established a high-school-to-college partnership in 1984. The "College Now" program provides numerous opportunities to students at different developmental stages, including the opportunity to earn a high school diploma and an associate's degree simultaneously. One of the more notable features of CUNY's program is that it offers college credit courses free of charge. Also significant is its commitment to underserved student populations. Of the 14,000 students enrolled in the College Now program in 2003, 22.2% were African American, 20.2% were white, 18.8% were Latino, and 20% were Asian. Also in 2003, 32.4% of New York City public high school students who enrolled in the CUNY system in 2003 participated in the College Now program.

Utah: The *New Century Scholarships Program*, created the Utah legislature in 1999, allows students to complete the requirements for an Associate's of Arts or Science degree while they are enrolled in high school. Students who complete the A.A. or A.S. degree by the fall following their high school graduation are then offered a scholarship that pays for 75% of their tuition at a Utah four-year college or university. The scholarship will be cancelled if a student fails to maintain a "B" average for two consecutive semesters. Since 2000, 270 students have earned an A.A. degree while in high school. Utah reimburses school districts $39.34 per credit to offset the dual enrollment programs. Utah's funding system is unique since the state, schools districts and postsecondary institutions all contribute towards the cost of dual enrollment programs. This means that students can access the program at no extra cost to them. Concurrent courses are offered at all of Utah's 109 high schools, 141 middle schools, and 10 state colleges, ensuring equitable access for all Utah high school students. Utah has also established six early college high schools to serve underrepresented or underachieving students interested in pursuing careers in math, science, or technology.

Washington: *The Running Start Program*, created by the legislature in 1990, allows students in 11th and 12th grades to take college-level courses at any of Washington's community and technical colleges, as well as Washington State, Eastern Washington, and Western Washington universities. This program allows students and the state to save money by reducing both the amount of time students spend in school and their college costs. It is estimated, that in 2001, parents saved $17.4 million in tuition and taxpayers saved $34.7 million because of the Running Start Program. It is also estimated, that in 2003-04, 9% of all high school students in Washington participated in the Running Start program. Of this percentage, 17% were students of color. Colleges are reimbursed by K-12 districts whose students participate in Running Start. (p. 4)

Financing Dual Enrollment Programs

A major concern for the states is financing the dual enrollment programs. The process is very complex, because the program has ties to both secondary and post secondary institutions. The states generally finance secondary education with Average Daily Attendance (ADA) funding, and postsecondary education with Full Time Equivalency (FTE) funds. In seven states, Alabama, Arkansas, California, Kansas, North Dakota, Oklahoma, and South Dakota, tuition for dual enrollment is paid for by the students. In six other states, Arizona, Missouri, Montana, Texas, Virginia, and West Virginia, the institutions that are participating in the program must agree whether they will pay the tuition or whether they will have the students pay.

When the institutions find it too expensive to fund the program themselves, or their priorities change, they then shift the burden to the students who would then have to pay for the tuition (Bailey, Fermin, Hughes & Karp, 2004).

In 11 states, tuition for the dual enrollment program is paid for by the participating institutions. These states include Colorado, Florida, Idaho, Iowa, Michigan, North Carolina, Ohio, Vermont, Washington, Wisconsin, and Wyoming. There are six states that provide state funding for the dual enrollment program—namely, Georgia, Illinois, Indiana, Maine, Minnesota, and Utah. This arrangement benefits students, secondary schools and postsecondary institutions (Bailey, Fermin, Hughes & Karp, 2004).

Some states have double funding, which means that neither high schools nor postsecondary institutions lose money, they both are funded by the state for high school students that are enrolled in the dual enrollment program (Boswell, 2001).

Other states have a combination of different policies. In North Carolina, students are responsible for books and fees, but the state pays the tuition. Whereas in other cases, both the secondary and postsecondary institution share the cost of tuition equally (Bailey, Fermin, Hughes & Karp, 2004).

Admissions Requirements

Some states like Arizona, Georgia, Idaho, Indiana, Iowa, and Montana will only admit juniors and seniors in their programs. Alabama, Arkansas, Ohio, and South Dakota allow students in Grades 9 through 12 to enroll in the programs.

Academic requirements for admission also differ from state to state. In some cases, students with advance standings are only allowed in the programs. Students must have high school grade point averages of 3.0 or above and Scholastic Aptitude Test scores of 1000 or better. Other academic criteria range from academically proficient to a combination of both advance and proficient, depending upon the courses that the students intend to take. Essentially, academic criteria are set by either the high schools or the postsecondary institutions or both (Bailey, Fermin, Hughes & Karp, 2004). In the state of Florida, these are the eligibility requirements set forth by the Florida Department of Education Dual Enrollment Program (2006):

- Be a student in a Florida public or nonpublic secondary school, or in a home education program
- For Florida public or nonpublic students, have a 3.0 unweighted grade point average to enroll in college credit courses, or a 2.0

unweighted grade point average to enroll in vocational certificate courses.
- Pass the appropriate section of the college placement test.
- Meet any additional admissions criteria set by the postsecondary institution (p.1).

Target Populations

According to Bailey, Fermin, Hughes & Karp, (2004), the states of California, Colorado, Florida, Kansas, Massachusetts New Hampshire, and North Carolina usually use the dual enrollment program for enrichment purposes, for students with special academic or vocational needs. Florida also promotes the program for advanced or gifted kids. On the other hand, in the states of Illinois, Missouri and Tennessee, only advanced students are targeted for the dual enrollment programs.

Program Intensity

Dual enrollment programs across the states vary in terms of structure and implementation. The program can also vary in terms of intensity, and according to researchers Bailey and Karp (2003), program intensity takes the form of the way in which students are exposed to numerous kinds of college-like experiences. These researchers developed three categories of intensity, which are as follows:

(a) Singleton programs, which refer to standalone college-level courses;
(b) Comprehensive programs, which subsume most of a student's academic experience; and
(c) Enhanced comprehensive programs, which offer students college course work coupled with nonacademic support such as counseling or mentoring to promote their success in postsecondary education (p. 13).

For the most part Singleton and Comprehensive programs are the ones primarily used to expose students to the dual enrollment program (Bailey & Karp, 2003).

Course Content

Courses in the dual enrollment programs are traditionally the same as regular college courses. Assignments and exams done by dually enrolled students are usually the same as those done by students in college, although in some instances there is a modified format (U.S. Department of Education, 2004). Postsecondary institutions usually approve syllabi and textbooks for courses.

Instructors

States usually require instructors in the dual enrollment program to have college credentials in the courses they are teaching. Instructors can be either college faculty or high school teachers. High school teachers teaching in the dual enrollment program must have the same qualifications as college faculty, and colleges reserve the right to approve all instructors teaching these courses (Bailey, Fermin, Hughes & Karp, 2004; Gomez, 2001).

Student Mix and Location

If dual enrollment courses are being taught in high schools, students attending are most likely high school students. When courses are taught on college campuses, the classes are a combination of college students and high school students (Bailey, Fermin, Hughes & Karp, 2004; Orr, 2002). Classes for dual enrollment can be taught on college campuses, on high school campuses or at home for students that are being home schooled. While in high school, some courses can be taught via video, television or the internet (Bailey, Fermin, Hughes & Karp, 2004; Hoffman, 2005; Orr, 2002).

Credits

According to Borrego (2001), on completion of dual enrollment courses, credit earned may be awarded immediately. However, in some cases credit is kept in escrow, until enrollment into a postsecondary institution. Then students are given credit for the courses they completed (Orr, 2002). In some states, transferring dual enrollment credits is a problem especially if the credits are to be transferred to a private postsecondary institution, (Hebert, 2001). Since there is no clear policy in place that governs the entire program in the United States, public and private four-year institutions may not accept dual enrollments credits if it is not state mandated or if the credits do not meet the minimum criteria of the institutions (Bailey et al, 2004; Clark, 2001; Del Genio & Johnstone, 2001; Orr, 2002).

State Policy

Many states like Florida, with dual enrollment programs make it mandatory for high schools to inform students of enrollment opportunities;

and colleges are obligated to accept credit transfers. However, there are fifteen states in which this information is considered voluntary (U.S. Department of Education, 2004). This means that information concerning this program, may or may not be passed on to students, and participation in the program is optional for high schools and colleges (Bailey, Fermin, Hughes & Karp, 2004).

The Impact of Accelerated Options on Minority Students

Researchers Hoffman and Vargas (2005) report that, "for low-income youth, first generation college goers, and students of color, unfulfilled aspirations to attend college can lead to dashed dreams" (p. 3). Hoffman and Vargas also contend that "only about half of those students who start college attain a Bachelor's degree. For students of color, the percentages are substantially worse" (p. 3). Krueger (2006) reports that there is "growing popularity and success of dual enrollment programs across the country" (p. 3). He also found that these programs are not reaching underrepresented students who would greatly benefit from them.

Kazis (2004) and other researchers challenge the public education system, both high schools and postsecondary institutions, to "double the number of young people from low-income and minority families who succeed in getting to and through postsecondary credential programs" (p. 1).

A study done by the National Center for Education Statistics, (NCES) and the U.S. Department of Education found that "among the estimated 2,050 institutions with dual enrollment programs, approximately 110 (5 percent) had dual enrollment programs specifically geared toward high school students at risk of education failure" (p.15). Of these institutions, 39% reported that the purpose of their dual enrollment programs was career/technical, 34% of the programs focused on academics, and 21% had a combination of career/technical and academics. Six percent of these programs had other agendas, such as career/technical (Kleiner & Lewis, 2005).

Summary

Although the dual enrollment program is an acceleration option that provides engaging opportunities for students from all walks of life, the review of the literature indicated that the program was not reaching those who would benefit from it the most: the low-income and underrepresented youth (Krueger, 2006). Research indicated that the dual enrollment program is having a minimal impact, on low-income and underrepresented students throughout the country. According to Krueger (2006) "schools with the highest minority enrollment were the least likely to offer dual enrollment courses when compared to schools with lower minority enrollment—58% to 78%" (p. 3).

Minority students are the fastest growing segment in our society, but they are the ones most likely to drop out of high school, and least likely to go to college according to Kazis (2004). More and more people are needed who are proficient in science and technology to meet the demands of our knowledge-based economy (Botstein, 2006). Yet, according to Botstein, not enough is being done in these areas to educate and graduate underrepresented students. The No Child Left Behind Act emphasizes "academic achievement for all youth, particularly those from groups traditionally underrepresented in postsecondary education" (Kazis, 2004, p. 6), but so far, there is still a significant gap between the white students and students from underrepresented groups.

The dual enrollment program has been very effective throughout the country among students who are academically successful and motivated (Krueger, 2006). It is less effective, however, for low-income and underrepresented students, who are not necessarily part of the program's targeted population (Hoffman, 2003). When given the opportunity to equally participate in this program, students of color, immigrant students, low-income students and first-generation college students adapt very well and benefit greatly from the program, according to Hoffman. Research has shown that students, including minorities, who participated in the State of Florida's dual enrollment program, were more likely to enroll in a post secondary institution than students who did not (Horne & Armstrong, 2006).

Chapter Three

METHODOLOGY

Introduction

This study investigated the impact of a dual enrollment program on the academic achievement of low-income and minority students. The procedures described in this chapter were designed to answer the three research questions that guided this study.

Research Question 1: How do low-income and minority high school students find out about the Dual Enrollment Program available to them?
Research Question 2: To what extent do low-income and minority high school students participate in their local Dual Enrollment Program?
Research Question 3: What is the success rate of low-income and minority high school students in their local Dual Enrollment Program?

Researchers surmised that part of the ongoing problem of senioritis results from a lack of connectivity between students and faculty, poor curriculum design, redundancy and repetition in coursework (Andrews & Davis, 2003; Blanchard, 1971; Hoffman & Robins, 2005). However, researchers Hoffman and Robins (2005), state that "educators also know that the education pipeline 'leaks' the most for those young people at the bottom of the income scale" (p. 5).

The Dual Enrollment Program is intended to provide a rigorous curriculum for all students, that will be used for both high school, and college preparation, that shortens the time for a college degree; and at the same time helps students bridge the gap between high school and college, while saving them money. It also proposes to bring about cohesive relationships between high schools and postsecondary institutions, and help reduce or alleviate students' remediation in college.

Research Design

This descriptive study examined the Dual Enrollment Program in a Coastal School District (CSD) in a southern state, through a survey that was given to the guidance counselors in five high schools in the county. Researchers Isaac and Michaels (1982), stated that the purpose for descriptive research is "to describe systematically the facts and characteristics of a given population or area of interest, factually and accurately" (p. 46). These researchers further stated that descriptive research "does not necessarily seek or explain relationships, test hypotheses, make predictions, or get at meanings and implications" (p.46). Descriptive research or survey research, as it is sometimes called, according to researchers Gall, Gall and Borg (2003) "have yielded much valuable knowledge about opinions, attitudes, and practices. This knowledge has helped shape educational policy and initiatives to improve existing conditions" (p. 290).

Selection of Participants

The target population for this study was the guidance counselors of five high schools in the county, who were responsible to inform and guide students with course selection and options, and career pathways, while they are in high school. Trend data of student admission, enrollment, and success of high school students, from 2003 to 2007 were used in conjunction with the counselors' responses to determine student success and achievement in the Dual Enrollment Program.

Instrumentation

A 13-item questionnaire with structured questions prepared by the researcher was given to the guidance counselors in five high schools in the county. The information that was gathered through the survey, and by follow-up interviews of guidance counselors, who supervise ninth through twelfth grade students enhanced the credibility of this research. Additionally, the researcher used archival data for students in the dual enrollment program, for the last four years, that was obtained, from the School District; to examine the overall participation and success rate of minority and low-income students in this program.

Procedures

A letter of intent was sent to the Superintendent of Public Schools of the Coastal School District asking permission to invite the selected high school guidance counselors, to voluntarily participate in a survey. Approval was given by the Supervisor of Guidance Counselors, and the Supervisor, Department of Measurement Data Analysis of the Coastal School District, to conduct the survey. The survey was used to gather information about the extent to which low-income and minority students in the local area high schools participate in the dual enrollment program. The survey was used to investigate the source (medium) through which these students are made aware of this program. Finally, it acquired information about the success rate of low-income and minority students in the dual enrollment program in the district in the last four years.

This permission was used to gain campus Institutional Review Board certification for the protection of participants. Following my oral proposal defense, a survey with a letter of informed consent was delivered to all guidance counselors in the five high schools, through the Supervisor, Department of Measurement and Data Analysis of the Coastal School District, requesting their participation. The completed surveys were then collected from the guidance counselors, by the Supervisor, Department of Measurement and Data Analysis and returned to the researcher for analysis.

Data Processing and Analysis

Data gathered from the survey was analyzed to acquire frequencies and percentages of the responses of the participants. A systematic method was used to organize the data into categories and patterns. The written analysis was supported by graphic representation to support the findings. There are limitations when conducting a qualitative research, because small samples cause concerns about their reliability and validity (Bogdan & Biklen, 1998). The interpretation of the data and subsequent conclusions were subject to opinions, prejudices and other biases of the researcher. However, to maintain objectivity throughout the entire process, a trusted colleague reviewed the data to assure objectivity in reporting.

Chapter Four

FINDINGS

Restatement of the Purpose

This study investigated the Dual Enrollment Program in a Coastal School District in a southern state, to determine the impact the program was having, on the academic achievement of low-income, and minority high school students. The study investigated the students' access to the program, their participation in the program, and their success rate while enrolled in the program, as measured by the judgments and perceptions of the guidance counselors of that school district, archival data, and input from personnel from the Community College, associated with that Coastal School District.

A survey prepared by the researcher, and approved by the Supervisor of Guidance Counselors, and the Supervisor, Department of Measurement and Data Analysis was distributed to guidance counselors in five high schools in a Coastal School District, by the Supervisor, Department of Measurement and Data Analysis; with instructions to return the completed survey to the said person by courier mail. Initially, guidance counselors who received the survey did not comply with the instructions of the Supervisor, Department of Measurement and Data Analysis, and the Supervisor of Guidance Counselors, to complete and return the survey. After three weeks, the survey was again sent out, to the guidance counselors of the five high schools in the CSD. Only four guidance counselors, out of a possible eighteen completed and returned the survey. Three of them were from Public Schools and the other one came from a Charter School. Results of the survey were reported pursuant to the three research questions that were investigated:

1. How do low-income and minority high school students find out about the Dual Enrollment program available to them?
2. To what extent do low-income and minority high school students participate in their local Dual Enrollment Program?
3. What is the success rate of low-income and minority high school students in their local Dual Enrollment Program?

The guidance counselors, who responded to the survey, were either, employed at a public school, or at a charter school in the Coastal School District. The answers to the survey questions numbers 2, and 3, indicated that all of them had attained a Master's Degree or higher education, and had an average of six years or more experience working as guidance counselors. It was further revealed by question 4 of the survey, that each guidance counselor was responsible for counseling an average of 500 high school students from 9th through 12th grades, each year. This answer was consistent for each guidance counselor who completed the survey. Question 5 of the survey referred to the acceleration options programs that were being offered to the students in the high schools. The guidance counselors for the two Public high schools indicated, that their schools offered the Advanced Placement, and the Dual Enrollment programs, but at the Charter school, the guidance counselor indicated that the Dual Enrollment program was the only acceleration option program offered at that school.

Research Question 1

How do low-income and minority high school students find out about the Dual Enrollment Program available to them?

In order to answer Research question 1 in the investigation, the survey looked at the responses the guidance counselors made to questions 6, 7, and 8. For question 6 of the survey, all of the guidance counselors indicated that students were informed about the Dual Enrollment Program through guidance counselors, teachers or administrators. The guidance counselor of the Charter school indicated that, postings in the school, and letters sent home to parents were other ways that the students were informed about the Dual Enrollment Program at their school. When the guidance counselors were asked if they routinely recommended the Dual Enrollment Program to students during Career Counseling, (question 7), all the guidance counselors in the Public school said no, but also said that they recommended it if the students met the qualifications or matched the students career goals. Guidance counselors in the Charter school routinely recommended the Dual Enrollment Program to students during Career Counseling. All the guidance

A Study of Dual Enrollment and Low-Income and Minority Students

counselors in the Public and Charter schools indicated that students were informed about the Dual Enrollment Program in 9th through 12th grades.

Table 4.1

Question 6: How are students informed about the Dual Enrollment Program?

School	Guidance Counselors	Teachers	Administrators	Other
Public	3	3	3	
Charter	1	1	1	1*

1* School Posters, and letters sent home to parents.

The information presented in Table 4.1 shows that the guidance counselors in the Public Schools indicated that students were informed about the Dual Enrollment Program by guidance counselors, teachers, and administrators. Whereas, the guidance counselor in the Charter School indicated that students were informed about the Dual Enrollment Program by guidance counselors, teachers, administrators, and also by posters in the school, and letters sent home to parents.

Table 4.2

Question 7: Is the Dual Enrollment Program routinely recommended to students during Career Counseling?

School	YES	NO
Public		3
Charter	1	

Based on the information shown in Table 4.2, the Dual Enrollment Program is not, routinely recommended to students during Career Counseling, by guidance counselors in the Public Schools. The guidance counselor in the Charter School indicated that the Dual Enrollment Program is routinely recommended to students during Career Counseling.

Table 4.3

Question 8: When are students informed about the Dual Enrollment Program at your school?

School	9th Grade	10th Grade	11th Grade	12th Grade	All Grades
Public					3
Charter					1

Based on the information shown in Table 4.3, the guidance counselors in the Public Schools, and the guidance counselors in the Charter School indicated that students are informed about the Dual Enrollment Program in all grades; 9th, 10th, 11th and 12th grades.

Research Question 2

To what extent do low-income and minority high school students participate in their local Dual Enrollment Program?

Questions 9 and 10 of the survey addressed the answer to the research Question 2 in the investigation. Guidance counselors in the Public schools indicated that less the 5% of students enrolled in the Dual Enrollment Program at their school were minority students. The guidance counselor in the Charter school indicted that 20% of the students enrolled in the Dual Enrollment program at the school were minority students.

When asked about the approximate number of minority students that were enrolled in the Dual Enrollment Program in the last four years (survey question 10), the guidance counselors in the Public high schools estimated between five and ten minority students. The guidance counselor in the Charter school indicated that there were approximately 25 minority students enrolled in the Dual Enrollment Program in the last four years.

Table 4.4

Question 9: Approximately what *percentage* of students enrolled in the Dual Enrollment Program at your school are minority students?

School	100%	75%	50%	20%	10%	Less than 5%
Public						3
Charter				1		

Based on the information presented in Table 4.4, the guidance counselors in the Public School estimate that less than 5% of the students enrolled in the Dual Enrollment Program at their school were minority students. The guidance counselor in the Charter School indicated that 20% of the students enrolled in the Dual Enrollment Program at her school were minority students.

Table 4.5

Question 10: During the past 4 years, approximately how many minority students, in your opinion have participated in the Dual Enrollment Program?

School	0-5	5-10	10-25	25-50	More than 50 Students
Public	2	1			
Charter			1		

Based on the information presented in Table 4.5, two guidance counselors from the Public Schools indicated that approximately 5 minority students have participated in the Dual Enrollment Program at their schools. One guidance counselor indicated that between 5 and 10 minority students have participated in the Dual Enrollment Program, at her school. The guidance counselor at the Charter School indicated that approximately 25 minority students have participated in the Dual Enrollment Program at her school in the past 4 years.

Research Question 3

What is the success rate of low-income and minority high school students in their local Dual Enrollment Program?

Question 12 of the survey addressed the success rate of the low-income and minority high school students enrolled in the Dual Enrollment Program, in a Coastal School District in a southern state. Guidance counselors in both Public and Charter high schools estimated that between 50% and 100% of low-income and minority students at their high school go on to college and are successful.

To complete the survey, question 12 asked if the Dual Enrollment Program was an effective acceleration option for bridging the gap between high school and college? All the guidance counselors agreed that it was. Overall, the survey investigating the awareness, participation and, success rate of low-income and minority students in the Dual Enrollment Program in a CSD showed that students were made aware of the program through guidance counselors, teachers and administrators; and additionally, through school postings and letters to parents, in the Charter school, in the 9th through 12th grades. Qualified minority high school students who participated in the program, averaged less than 5% in the Public school, and 20% in the Charter school. It is worth mentioning that the Dual Enrollment Program was the only acceleration option program offered at the Charter school, which probably accounts for the higher participation rate of low-income and minority students in the program, at that school. Also, the success rate of low-income and minority high school students who participated in the Dual Enrollment Program, was between 50% to 100%, both in the Public schools and the Charter school.

Table 4.6

Question 12: What percentage of minority students in the Dual Enrollment Program from your school go on to college?

School	100%	50%	25%	10%	Less than 10%
Public	1	2			
Charter	1				

Based on the information presented in Table 4.6, guidance counselors in the Public School indicated that between 50% to 100% of minority students that participate in the Dual Enrollment Program, at their schools go on to college. The guidance counselor in the Charter School indicated that 100% of the minority students that participated in the program went on to college.

Table 4.7

Question 11: The Dual Enrollment Program is an effective acceleration option for bridging the gap between high school and college.

School	Strongly Disagree	Disagree	Neutral	Agree	Strongly Agree
Public				3	
Charter				1	

Based on the information in Table 4.7 presented above, guidance counselors from the Public Schools and the Private Schools all agree that the Dual Enrollment Program is an effective acceleration option for bridging the gap between high school and college.

Interview

Other findings from this investigation were obtained through a telephone interview, of the Student Development Advisor at the Community College associated with the Coastal School District (CSD). This researcher asked about the development and progression of the Dual Enrollment Program; and the nature of the collaboration, between the Community College, and the Coastal School District. The Advisor revealed that the program was being avidly promoted, by the Community College, as a viable option for high schools students. The advisor indicated that part of the promotion for this program included an annual conference with Guidance counselors of all Public High Schools in the area, being serviced by the Community College. Parents of students who were being Home Schooled, and delegates from Private Schools were also invited to attend the conference. This Advisor indicated that the last conference that was held last October, attracted over 350 people. This researcher also inquired about the payment of tuition and books for the dual enrollment program in this CSD. The Advisor for the Community College indicated that tuition was waived for all students in the program, and was paid for by the State; The cost of Textbooks for students in Public and Charter high schools were paid for by the Coastal School District. However, textbooks for students attending Private Schools, and textbooks for students being home schooled, were paid for by their parents.

The Student Development Advisor at the Community College said that for the last four years, there had been a drastic increase of students participating in the Dual Enrollment Program from the CSD. The Advisor also said that the latest statistics for the Program showed that 12% of the overall CSD school population were participating in the Dual Enrollment Program, which is approximately 11,000 students. The Student Development Advisor was not able to comment on the minority population, in the DE program, nor on their success rate, as it applies to the CSD, saying that that information was not readily available to her. The Advisor seemed pleased at the overall success that the DE Program is having in the CSD.

Archival Data

In addition to the information gathered through the survey, and the interviews, archival data for the Dual Enrollment Program, for the 2005-2006 school year was also examined. The following Table 4.8 (below) shows the rates of penetration of the Dual Enrollment Program, by Colleges, and by counties in the southern state for the 2005-06 school year. As indicated by the table, the CSD had 1,329 students in the program, which was 12.38% of the 11th and 12th grade population of the School District at that time. Table 4.9 (below) shows the Dual Enrollment rates of penetration by race/ethnicity in the different counties during the 2005-06 school. This table shows that White students made up 13.81%, African American students made up 3.04%, and Hispanics Students made of 6.27% of the populations of qualified students in the program at that time from the CSD.

The goal for examining the archival data was to get a more accurate representation of student participation and, student success, by county, in the Dual Enrollment Program, in this southern state

Table 4.8 Dual Enrollment Penetration Study Rates of Penetration in Dual Enrollment by College, 2005-06

College	Dual Enrollment Headcount	Dual Enrollment Penetration Rate All Students
Brevard	2,764	26.57%
Broward	1,742	4.88%
Central Florida	1,107	13.89%
Chipola	411	19.02%
Daytona Beach	1,082	10.93%
Edison	1,364	7.33%
Florida CC @ Jax	1,645	10.52%
Florida Keys	306	27.47%
Gulf Coast	2,063	48.99%
Hillsborough	1,080	4.63%
Indian River	1,823	18.39%
Lake City	443	17.54%
Lake-Sumter	461	8.17%
Manatee	1,329	12.38%
Miami Dade	1,617	3.45%
North Florida	308	15.98%
Okaloosa-Walton	559	10.54%
Palm Beach	1,772	7.79%
Pasco-Hernando	1,301	13.39%
Pensacola	1,912	21.32%
Polk	841	7.98%
St. Johns	735	7.56%
St. Petersburg	1,604	10.71%
Santa Fe	681	13.88%
Seminole	465	5.01%
South Florida	925	36.35%
Tallahassee	998	18.43%
Valencia	1,578	5.45%
System	32,916	9.69%
Minimum	306	3.45%
Maximum	2,764	48.99%

NUMERATOR=Dual Enrollment student headcount by race/ethnicity, 2005-06, Florida Community College Student Data Base

DENOMINATOR=Public school membership by race/ethnicity in grades 11 and 12, Fall 2005, Education Information and Accountability Service.

Table 4.9 Dual Enrollment Rates of Penetration by Race/Ethnicity, 2005-06

College	Dual Enrollment Penetration Rate White Students	African American Students	Hispanic Students
Brevard	28.47%	16.81%	25.90%
Broward	7.08%	1.77%	4.54%
Central Florida	16.27%	5.16%	7.66%
Chipola	22.38%	6.42%	9.52%
Daytona Beach	12.23%	5.07%	8.08%
Edison	9.70%	2.56%	2.89%
Florida CC @ Jax	10.11%	3.65%	4.45%
Florida Keys	31.09%	4.76%	24.42%
Gulf Coast	54.33%	19.62%	45.45%
Hillsborough	6.41%	2.53%	2.64%
Indian River	22.01%	8.39%	12.93%
Lake City	20.38%	2.72%	8.06%
Lake-Sumter	9.68%	2.79%	6.28%
Manatee	13.81%	3.04%	6.27%
Miami Dade	4.72%	1.95%	3.38%
North Florida	21.76%	4.71%	14.75%
Okaloosa-Walton	11.76%	2.98%	9.47%
Palm Beach	9.91%	5.20%	5.14%
Pasco-Hernando	14.07%	5.15%	9.81%
Pensacola	26.13%	4.37%	20.36%
Polk	10.39%	2.87%	4.05%
St. Johns	8.24%	2.78%	7.52%
St. Petersburg	12.75%	2.31%	5.00%
Santa Fe	18.66%	4.39%	15.69%
Seminole	5.44%	2.27%	3.31%
South Florida	38.52%	34.61%	28.83%
Tallahassee	23.98%	7.87%	25.14%
Valencia	7.67%	2.21%	3.78%
System	13.56%	3.70%	4.80%
Minimum	4.72%	1.77%	2.54%
Maximum	54.33%	34.61%	45.45%

NUMERATOR=Dual Enrollment student headcount by race/ethnicity, 2005-06, Florida Community College Student Data Base

DENOMINATOR=Public school membership by race/ethnicity in grades 11 and 12, Fall 2005, Education Information and Accountability Service

Chapter Five

SUMMARY, CONCLUSIONS, AND RECOMMENDATIONS

Summary

This study investigated the impact of a dual enrollment program on the academic achievement of low-income and minority students in a Coastal School District, in a southern state. The data gathered for this study were obtained through a survey, an interview, and archival student achievement data.

In Chapter One, the background information stated that low-income and minority students were not necessarily the targeted population of the dual enrollment program. Research indicates that the majority of students dropping out of high school come from the underrepresented populations, students of color, students whose first language is not English, and students from low-income families (Kazis, 2004). Researchers also found that students drop out of high school in the eleventh and twelfth grades, because they are bored and disengaged, a phenomenon more specifically referred to as senioritis. This senioritis is mainly caused by repetition of coursework, poor curriculum design and a lack of connectivity between students and faculty (Andrews & Davis, 2003).

The dual enrollment program offers students the opportunity to simultaneously, earn high school, and college credits, while still in high school, and helps with the transition of high school to college. It also addresses senioritis, savings on college tuition, and remediation courses in college. The purpose of the study was to determine the impact of a dual enrollment program on the academic achievement of low-income and minority students on a Coastal School District, by answering three questions: How do low-income and minority high school students find out about the dual enrollment program available to them? To what extent do low-income and minority high school students participate in their local dual enrollment program? And what is the success rate of low-income and minority student high school students in their local dual enrollment program?

Chapter Two presented an extensive review of the literature of the dual enrollment program as an effective acceleration option program for high school students. The review examined the program from its inception, through its progression to what it represents today. The dual enrollment program offers high school students the opportunity to build a college transcript that increases their chances of graduating from high school, and going on to college to graduate with a baccalaureate degree. The program is structured to challenge motivated students, while saving them money and bridging the gap between high school and college. The program also encourages collaboration and partnerships between high schools, and postsecondary institutions.

Chapter Three described the methodology that was being used to obtain data on the impact that the dual enrollment program was having, on the academic achievement of low-income and minority students in a Coastal School District. Data for this investigation was obtained, using a survey that was given to guidance counselors of five high schools, an interview of the Student Development Advisor of the Community College, and archival data showing the status of the dual enrollment program in the CSD.

Chapter Four, gave us an insight into the perceptions, and observations of the guidance counselors regarding three areas of interest: the medium through which low-income and minority students find out about the dual enrollment program, how well they participate, and perform in the program and the success rate they have in the program.

The results of a telephone interview with the Student Development Advisor of the Community College associated with the CSD, revealed that over the last few years, the dual enrollment program was being avidly promoted as a viable option for high school students by the Community College, and that there was mutual collaboration between the CSD and the Community College. This collaboration included division of responsibilities for books and tuition, and other support provided for students in the program. The Advisor indicated that part of this promotion included an annual Conference with Guidance Counselors of all the Public High Schools in the area, parents of students that were Home Schooled, and delegates from Private Schools. This advisor also noted that there had been an increase of student participation in the program over the last four years in the district. Archival data showed the penetration rate of the dual enrollment program, in the CSD in terms of race/ethnicity, and overall student participation. This data obtained from this southern state, revealed that a comparison of the dual enrollment penetration rates was done for the 2005-2006 school year, for Whites, African Americans and Hispanics students enrolled in the program. It showed that from the Coastal School District, 13.81 % of the students were White, 3.04% were African American, and 6.27% were Hispanics. This indicates that there is a significant disparity between the number of whites students, and the number of minority students who are enrolled in the dual enrollment program, in the Coastal School District.

The overall findings of this investigation revealed that all students, including low-income and minority students, were being informed about the dual enrollment program, from the 9th through the 12th grades. It also showed that low-income and minority students were participating in the program, and that between 50% and 100% of these students who participated in the program were successful, and went on to college. The findings also revealed, that the dual enrollment program has been diligently promoted in recent years, through collaboration of the Community College and the Coastal School District.

Conclusions

Research indicates that the dual enrollment program, when implemented properly can be a solution for senioritis, a bridge between high school and college, a way for students and parents to save money on the cost of college, and an opportunity for policymakers to have a well-educated workforce. Researcher Kruger (2006), said that, "dual enrollment increases academic performance and educational attainment." Boswell (2001) said that the dual enrollment program is a way of "fostering collaboration between high school and colleges, resulting in reduced redundancy and ensuring a more seamless K-16 public education system. Hebert (2001) added that through this program parents save substantially on tuition, books, and transportation for their children. By all accounts, it seems that with adequate promotion, and commitment from all stakeholders, the dual enrollment program can be a catalyst that successfully moves students from high school through college, especially the ones who need it the most; the low-income, and minority students. Researcher Hugo (2001) contends that, "dual enrollment provides a long-term strategy to improve the preparation of minority students so that they will be competitive for college admission." However, research also indicates that the program is not geared to helping the low-income and minority students who have the highest percentage of high school drop out rates in the country, and who would benefit from the program the most, both socially, and economically (Kazis,2004).

This investigation focused on the impact of the dual enrollment program, on the academic achievement of low-income and minority students, in a Coastal School District in a southern state. It must also be noted that this southern state has one of the most successful dual enrollment programs in the country; which emphasizes collaboration between school districts and postsecondary institutions, and student achievement. This state also has a highly sophisticated public school system that can track students from kindergarten through college.

Through the results of the survey, the investigation revealed, that all high school students in the CSD, in Public and Charter schools, whether they were white or minority, were being informed about the program through guidance counselors, teachers, administrators, and sometimes through school posters, and letters sent home to parents. The investigation also indicated that low-income and minority students were participating in the program, and through this participation, 50% to 100% of these students were successful, and went on to college.

According to the Student Development Advisor of the Community College the dual enrollment program in the CSD has been avidly promoted through yearly conferences with guidance counselors, and parents of home schooled students; and through open communication with other officials of the CSD. The result of this cooperation between the Community College and the CSD, as perceived by the Advisor is a notable increase in student participation and student achievement in this program in the last four years.

Feedback from guidance counselors, through the survey, and the interview of the Student Development Advisor of the Community College was quite positive about the state of the dual enrollment program in this school district. However, archival data showed that there was a significant disparity between the participation, and success rate of white students as compared to minority student, in the dual enrollment program. The question then is why is there such a disparity between whites and minorities students, in a state that purports to have one of the best dual enrollment program in the country; and has a tracking system that is unsurpassed by no other?

There can be several significant internal, and external factors that may be having an impact on the results of this investigation. For example, research indicates that the dual enrollment program is not geared to accommodate low-income and, minority students (Krueger, 2006), mostly because of low grade point average in school, which disqualifies them from the program. Research also suggests, that part of the problem lies with lack of parental involvement, and support of their children in high school. Parents of minority children, who may never have gone to college, tend to be less likely to encourage their children to take courses in school, that are more challenging, and that might qualify them to participate in the dual enrollment program (Welner, 2008). Another factor that may be influencing the disparity may be that students are not informed about the dual enrollment program early on, during Career Counseling with the Guidance Counselors, which can greatly influence the pathways students take during their time in high school.

Research has also found that the involvement of the local Community College plays an important role in promoting and advancing the dual enrollment program in area high schools. Programs such as The High School Principals' Council, in which high school Principals regularly meet with representatives of the Community College is a medium for collaboration and cooperation between high schools and the local Community College. The agendas for these meetings usually center around ways by which the College and the high schools can work together, and build real partnerships with each other (Helfgot, 2001). Other promotions by the Community College are Joint College Night, an annual event, whereby parents and students are given the opportunity to meet with representatives of several major colleges, and universities, and preview their offerings, and attend some of their workshops. And also, Senior Preview Day, where high school students take part in mini classes, and a program fair involving academic programs, and a tour of the Community College. This gives students a better insight into all the options that are available to them, which can assist them in making right choices that can influence their future undertakings (Helfgot, 2001).

High School guidance counselors in the Coastal School District, and representatives from the Community College, who perceive the dual enrollment program as advantageous for students and, who have seen a recent increase in the rate of student participation, and success as positive need to evaluate the research. Their duty as students' representatives is to determine, why the archival data shows a drastic disparity of participation and success rate, between white students and minority students in the district. A complete examination of the program in the CSD, by all stakeholders, and an introduction of some of the previously mentioned best practices of successful programs, may be able to address the problems, and could lead to a more equitable distribution of student participation, and success in the program in this district.

Implications for Practice

This study investigated the impact of the Dual Enrollment Program on the academic achievement of low-income and minority high school students in a CSD in a southern state, based on the perceptions of high school guidance counselors, the Student Development Advisor of the Community College, and archival data. The implications that are noted are as follows:

1. Use this Coastal School District as an example, to demonstrate how a dual enrollment program can be economically sound, by saving parents and students thousands of dollars in college tuition and books; improving high school and college graduation rates, and producing a well-educated work force.
2. Use the student participation and success data of the district, to draw up an action plan that would remedy the disparity of white students to minority students in the program; that truly represents a cross section of the students in the district.
3. Create a plan that will encourage parents of minority students to become more involved in their children's education.
4. Provide training to parents, so that they could monitor, their children' progress and participation in the program throughout their time in high school.
5. Encourage stakeholders to visit other school districts with successful programs, to monitor and emulate their success strategies.
6. Use the student participation and success data, to overhaul the dual enrollment program in the CSD, and in so doing identify its weaknesses and its strengths.
7. Use the data derived from this study, to create better relationships between the high schools and the Community College; by having Principals play a more active role in the preservation of the program.

Implications for Research

Based on the revelations in this investigational research, on the impact of dual enrollment program of low-income and other minority students on student achievement, this researcher recommends the following for use in future, and perhaps in more extensive studies:

1. Conduct a full length study of the health and condition of the dual enrollment program; throughout this southern state, by expanding

this research, and paying particular attention to the enrollment, participation and success rate of low-income and minority students.
2. Since many of the guidance counselors in the CSD refused to respond to the survey, then an annual survey of high school guidance counselors should be conducted to follow up and monitor improvements, and any changes in the dual enrollment program.
3. Do a follow up interview with representatives of the Community College, to gain insight into valuable information that may enhance the program, and increase more student participation.

Recommendations

An implication of this study is that the dual enrollment program, when implemented properly in a school district, can be an effective mechanism for addressing, senioritis, bridging the gap between high school to college, saving parents and students thousands of dollars in college expenses, and producing a workforce of educated individuals to compete in our global economy. Imagine one program that can accomplish all these positive outcomes.

It is therefore, recommended, that the implications listed above be considered. After conducting the investigation of the impact that the dual enrollment program was having on the achievement of low-income and minority students, in a CSD, this researcher found that the program is having a positive effect on these students. The investigation revealed that the low-income and minority students who qualified for, and, were taking part in the program were having average to better than average success in the program, as reported by guidance counselors. However, the disparity between the number of white, and minority students taking part in the program was significant, and needs improving.

It is impossible to predict the fate, and future of minority students, eligible to participate and succeed in the dual enrollment program, even with everything being equal. Under the circumstances, the possibilities are endless, if and, when these recommendations are adhered to, in this Coastal School District. There is the potential to have and maintain a strong dual enrollment program that will be beneficial and accessible to all students in the district.

REFERENCES

Andrews, H.A., & Davis, J. (August, 2003). When high school is not enough. *The American School Board Journal.* Retrieved April 10, 2005, from http://www.asbj.com

AP Central (2002). Humble Beginnings. Retrieved February 3, 2005, from http://www.collegeboard.org

Bailey, T. R., & Karp, M. M. (2003). Promoting college access and success: A review of dual credit and other high school/college transition programs. *Community College Research Center, Teachers College.* Retrieved January 12, 2007, from http://www.tc.edu/ccrc

Bailey, T. R., Hughes, K. L., & Karp, M. M. (2003). Dual enrollment programs: Easing transitions from high school to college. *Community College Research Center.* Retrieved, May 15, 2006, from http://www.tc.edu/ccrc

Bailey, T. R., Fermin, B., Hughes, K. L., & Karp, M. M. (2004). State Dual enrollment Policies: Addressing Access and Quality. Report prepared for the Office of Vocational and Adult Education, U.S. Department of Education *Community College Research Center.* Retrieved April 10, 2005, from http://www.tc.edu/ccrc

Blanchard, B. E. (1971). *A national survey of curriculum articulation between the colleges of liberal arts and the secondary school.* Chicago: De Paul University.

Bogdan, R., & Biklen, S. (1998). *Qualitative research for education: An introduction to theory and method* (3rd ed.). Boston, MA: Allyn & Bacon.

Borrego, A. (2001). For many for-profit colleges, the transfer-of-credit blues. *Chronicle of Higher Education.* Retrieved, October 10, 2005, from http://www.chronicle.com

Boswell, K. (2001). State policy and postsecondary enrollment options: Creating seamless systems. *New Directions for Community Colleges,* 113, 7-14.

Botstein, L. (2006). The trouble with high school. *The School Administrator*, Retrieved July 6, 2007, from http://www.aasa.org

Brawer, F. B., & Cohen, A.M. (2003). *The American community college* (4th ed.). San Francisco: Jossey-Bass.

Brush, S. (2005). Credit-transfer rules weighted in congress. *Chronicle of Higher Education*. Retrieved, October 10, 2005, from http://www.chronicle.com

Carnegie Commission on Higher Education (1971). Continuity and discontinuity: Higher education and the schools. In L.B. Mayhew (Ed.), *The carnegie commission on higher education* (pp. 93-98). San Francisco: Jossey-Bass.

Clark, R.W. (2001). Dual credit: a report of progress and policies that offer high school students' college credits. *The Pew Charitable Trusts*. Retrieved June 21, 2006, from http://www.pewtrusts.com

Del Genio, B., & Johnstone, B. (2001). College-level learning in high school: Purposes, policies and practical implications. *Association of American Colleges and Universities*. Retrieved October 15, 2006, from http://www.aacu-edu.org

Education Commission of the States (2001). Postsecondary options: Dual / concurrent enrollment. Retrieved October 15, 2006, from http://www.ecs.org

Florida Department of Education, K20, The Education Data Warehouse (2007, July). Fast facts: Student success series #2007-06 dual enrollment penetration study. Retrieved, September 6, 2008, from www.fldoe.org/cc

Florida's Dual Enrollment Program (n.d.). Retrieved May 6, 2006, from http://www.fldoe.org/cc

Gall, M.D., Gall, J.P., & Borg, W.R., (2003). *Educational research: An introduction* (7th ed.). Boston: Allyn & Bacon.

Gehring, J. (2001). Dual-enrollment programs spreading. *Education Week*. 20, 17-18.

Gomez, G.G. (2001). Sources and information: Creating effective collaboration between high schools and community colleges. *New Directions for Community College*, 113, 81-86.

Greenberg, A.R., (1989). *Concurrent enrollment programs: college credits for high school students*. Bloomington: Phi Delta Kappa Education Foundation.

Hauptman, A.M. (2004). Using institutional incentives to improve student performance. In R. Kazis, J. Vargas & N. Hoffman (Eds.), *Double the numbers, increasing post secondary credentials for underrepresented youth* (pp. 213-220). Harvard Educational Press, Cambridge: MA.

Hebert, L. (2001). A comparison of learning outcomes for dual-enrollment mathematics students taught by high school teachers versus college faculty. *Community College Review,* Retrieved June 2, 2005, from http://www.crw.sagepub.com

Helfgot, S.R. (2001). Concurrent enrollment and more: Elements of a successful partnership. *New Directions for Community Colleges,* 113, 43-49.

Hoffman, N. (2003). College credit in high school: Increasing college attainment rates, for underrepresented students. *Change.* Retrieved, July 8, 2007, from http://www.change.org

Hoffman, N. (2004) Challenge, not remediation: The early college high school initiative. In R. Kazis, J. Vargas & N. Hoffman (Eds.), *Double the numbers: Increasing postsecondary credentials for underrepresented youth* (pp. 213-220). Harvard Education Press, Cambridge: MA.

Hoffman, N., & Vargas, J. (2005). Early college high school initiative integrating Grades 9 through 14: State policies to support and sustain early college high schools. *Jobs for the Future.* Retrieved February 8, 2007, from http://www.jff.org

Hoffman, N. (2005). Add and subtract: Dual enrollment as a state strategy to increase postsecondary success for underrepresented students. *Jobs for the Future.* Retrieved June 21, 2006, from http://www.jff.org

Hoffman, N., & Robbins, A. (2005). Head start on college: Dual enrollment strategies in new england 2004-2005. *Jobs for the future.* Retrieved October 5, 2006, from http://www.jff.org

Horne, J., & Armstrong, J.D. (2004). Dual enrollment students are more likely to enroll in postsecondary education. *Florida Department of Education K20.* Retrieved Retrieved April 8, 2007, from http://www.fldoe.org/cc

Horne, J., & Armstrong, J. D. (2006). Community college dual enrollment students do well in subsequent university courses. *Florida Department of Education K20. Florida's dual enrollment program.* Retrieved June 21, 2008, from http://www.fldoe.org/cc

Hugo, E. B. (2001). Dual enrollment for underrepresented student populations. *New Directions for Community Colleges.* 113, 67-72.

Isaac, S., & Michael, W. B., (1982). *Handbook in research and evaluation: For educational and behavioral sciences.* (2nd. Ed.). San Diego: EdITS/Educational And Industrial Testing Services.

Kazis, R. (2004). Introduction. In Kazis, R., Vargas, J. & Hoffman, N. (Eds.), *Double the numbers: Increasing postsecondary credentials for underrepresented youth.* Cambridge: Harvard Education Press.

Kleiner, B., & Lewis, L. (2005). *Dual enrollment of high school students at postsecondary institution: 2002-0. (NCES) 2005-008).* U.S. Department of Education. Washington, DC: National Center for Education Statistics.

Krueger, C. (2006). Dual/concurrent enrollment. *ECS Policy Brief.* Retrieved June 21, 2006, from http://www.ecs.org

Orr, M.T. (2002, January). *Dual enrollment: developments, trends and impacts*. Paper presented to the Community College Research Center. Teachers College Columbia University. New York, N.Y.

Orr, M.T. (2003). Shaping postsecondary transitions: influences of the national academic foundation career academy. *IEE Briefs, Journal Articles Evaluative Reports. April, 2003*. Retrieved, August 10, from http://www.

Rodrigues, D. (2004). Making the most of a university/high school partnership: University park campus school. In R. Kazis, J. Vargas & N. Hoffman (Eds.), *Double the numbers: Increasing postsecondary credentials for underrepresented youth* (pp. 197-204). Harvard Education Press, Cambridge: MA.

Smith, J. D. (2003). *Dual enrollment as an educational acceleration option for a high minority, low performing high school*. Unpublished doctoral dissertation. Argosy University, Florida.

The High School Leadership Summit, (2005). *Dual enrollment: Accelerating the transition to college*. Retrieved June 25, from http://www.ed.gov

United States Department of Health and Human Services (2008). *Federal TRIO programs 2008 annual low income levels*. Retrieved September 20, 2008, from http://www.hhs.gov

Vargas, J. (2004). Dual enrollment: Lessons from Washington and Texas. In R. Kazis J. Vargas & N. Hoffman (Eds.), *Double the Numbers: Increasing postsecondary credentials for underrepresented youth* (pp. 205-212). Harvard Education Press, Cambridge: MA.

Walthers, K., & Robinson, J. (2006). Concurrent enrollment: Funding in Utah. *Center for Public Policy and Administration*. Retrieved March 18, 2008, from http://www.cppa.edu/publication/higher

Wells, A., & Serna, I., (1996). The politics of culture: Understanding local political resistance to detracking in racially mixed schools. *The Harvard Education Review*, 66, 93-117.

Windham, P. (1997). High school and community college dual enrollment: issues of rigor and transferability. ERIC clearinghouse on educational management. (ERIC Document Reproduction Service No. ED413936). Retrieved June 6, 2007, from http://www.eric.ed.gov

APPENDIXES

APPENDIX A

SURVEY

Survey

Dual Enrollment Program Study

Dear Participant,

This survey is intended to gather information about how students find out about a district's Dual Enrollment Program, the extent to which students participate in the program and the eventual success students have in the program at your high school. The survey should take approximately 15 minutes. Thank you for your cooperation. To assure confidentiality, as noted in the cover letter, no individually identifiable data will be reported. All information will be kept in a secured location and will be destroyed upon completion of the study.

School Name: _____

Check all that apply

1. My school is a

    ____ Public School
    ____ Charter School

2. I have worked as a guidance counselor for

    ____ 1-3 years
    ____ 4-6 years
    ____ 7-10 years
    ____ More than 10 years

3. I have my

    ____ Bachelor's Degree
    ____ Master's Degree
    ____ Doctorate
    ____ other (certificates) _____

4. Each school year, I counsel/advise approximately ____ students in

    ____ 9th grade

_____ 10th grade
_____ 11th grade
_____ 12th grade
_____ All of the above

5. Program options at my school include

   _____ Advanced Placement (AP)
   _____ International Baccalaureate (IB)
   _____ Dual Enrollment
   _____ Other (please specify)

6. How are students informed about the Dual Enrollment program? (Check all that apply)

   _____ Guidance Counselors
   _____ Teachers
   _____ Administrators
   _____ Other (Please Specify)

7. Is the Dual Enrollment Program routinely recommended to students during Career Counseling?

   _____ Yes
   _____ No

8. When are students informed about the Dual Enrollment Program at your school?

   _____ 9th Grade
   _____ 10th Grade
   _____ 11th Grade
   _____ 12th Grade
   _____ All of the above

9. Approximately what percentage of students currently enrolled in the Dual Enrollment Program at your school are minority students?

   _____ 100%
   _____ 75%

_____ 50%
_____ 10%
_____ Less than 5%

10. During the past 4 years, approximately how many minority students, in your opinion have participated in the Dual Enrollment Program?

   _____ 0-5 students
   _____ 5-10 students
   _____ 10-25 students
   _____ 25-50 students
   _____ More than 50 students

11. The Dual Enrollment Program is an effective acceleration option for bridging the gap between high school and college

   _____ Strongly Disagree
   _____ Disagree
   _____ Neutral
   _____ Agree
   _____ Strongly Agree

   I think _____ is a more viable option for students.

12. What percentage of minority students in the Dual Enrollment Program from your high school go on to college?

   _____ 100%
   _____ 50%
   _____ 25%
   _____ 10%
   _____ Less than 10%

13. May I contact you with any follow up questions, if needed?

   _____ Yes
   _____ No

Your Name (Optional)_____
Contact Number_____

APPENDIX B

INTERVIEW

Interview

Interview Questions for Student Development Advisor Community College

Interview Questions for the Student Development Advisor at the Community College.

1. What is your official Title?

2. Do you oversee the Dual Enrollment Program (DE) at the Community College?

3. What is the state of the Dual Enrollment Program in the Coastal School District (CSD)?

4. How is the Dual Enrollment being promoted in the CSD?

5. How were school officials, parents, and students being informed about the DE Program?

6. How is the DE Program being financed in the CSD?

7. Is there a growing minority population in the DE program? If so, what is the participation rate, and success rates of these students?

8. What is the overall response about the DE Program, from school officials, parents, and students?

9. What is the student population in the DE Program at this time?

10. In the last four years, have you seen an increase of awareness, and participation in the DE Program in the CSD?

Edwards Brothers Malloy
Oxnard, CA USA
November 25, 2013